Never Alone

A.J. Piatkowski

ISBN 978-1-0980-9088-3 (paperback)
ISBN 978-1-0980-9089-0 (digital)

Christian Faith Publishing
832 Park Avenue
Meadville, PA 16335
www.christianfaithpublishing.com

All biblical references come from NIV version.

Printed in the United States of America

Chapter 1

Power in the Tongue, Proverbs 18:21

September 29, 2010

omans 8:28. I am seventy-years-old and have been legally divorced for almost ten years.

This book is not meant to cause harm to my ex-husband. Instead, it is only meant to help and encourage believers that God is with you in everything, at all times, even in a divorce, though it is his will that his children never have to experience any.

I had been married for thirty-two years. Most of it was abusive and controlling in every way imaginable. In fact, after ten years of marriage, I had filed for divorce.

We were both Christians. After some Christian counseling and many flowers, we decided to reconcile even though my gut told me no. I believed I was doing the Christian things—that I should forgive as God forgave me, seventy times seven.

Things went fairly well for a few years, but old behaviors slowly crept in. Eventually, we were back to square one, and things got even worse than before.

After my husband lost his job due to illness, we had to resort to government disability, which took us three years to receive. I was forced to sell my wedding ring, a 1980 show Corvette, and had depleted my 401(k) just to keep afloat.

Through all the stress, he decided he could no longer attend church. He reasoned that he did not want to get sick in church and be embarrassed. After that, things really went downhill.

I continued to work at a local aircraft factory. I had been there twenty-eight years. It had become a place of refuge, a place I could feel safe and have peace.

My husband's days were spent doing home hobbies, watching television, and becoming increasingly angry, which I became the brunt of.

I resigned myself of any hope in the marriage. I prayed God would take one of us home. That didn't happen.

I wanted a divorce, but he convinced me I would lose everything, including my dogs, which were my only friends, be destined to homeless, and be alone for the rest of my life. Any self-esteem I had was long gone. I had given up on myself, but God had a plan.

The Decision

One weekend, my widowed mother came for a visit. We were all sitting on the porch when my husband informed my mother that if she wanted to live with us, she couldn't park her two cars on the street in front of the house. He also informed her they would be sold, and a mechanic friend and he would split the profits. My mother never had a desire to live with us, but that was my *light bulb* moment. Right then, I told him I wanted a divorce, and we stopped talking. I no longer cared about my future; I just knew I didn't want to spend the rest of my life like this.

Every day after work, I would grab something from a drive-through to eat, go home, and lock myself and four dogs—three rottweilers and a terrier—in the bedroom till the next morning, when I went back to work, praying continuously that the Lord would show me what to do. That went on for two months.

My faith wavered since I saw no solutions. Fear set in. Having three Rottweilers wasn't much comfort since they were also afraid of him.

One evening I was in the garage, my husband came up behind me as if he were in a trance and started choking me. I started to black-out. I swung back and hit him where it counted.

He said, "If you ever do that again, I must knock you on your ass," and steadily walked back into the house.

Things were getting more violent. He knocked a hole in the bedroom door. One day, I came home and he had torn the television cables set of the bedroom wall, and the landline phone wires were also gone.

God had told me it was time. The next day after work, I went to the Women's Crisis Center still wondering if somehow this was my fault. They gave me a test of questions for me to answer. All of my answers were yes. Yes is not a good answer in this situation. I will never forget the look on their faces. They recommended that I immediately go to the courthouse and file a restraining order for my safety.

The judge signed the restraining order. I took it to the closest precinct by my house. They followed me home and removed him from the premises. That was August 10, 2010.

After he left, he went to the bank and clean out the checking account.

I really didn't realize how awful my abuse was, or maybe I was in denial. I had been so desensitized that I had learned to accept it. I had no self-esteem, no friend, but I had God. "He restoreth my soul" (Psalm 23:3).

I didn't understand why I had to wait two months. Looking back, I understand. As they say, "Timing is everything." And God's timing is perfect.

If I would not have waited on God, I know it would not have turned out the way it did. It was the perfect plan falling into place.

He was gone and the house was so peaceful. Even the dogs could relax.

I was afraid he might retaliate. I double-locked all my doors.

I clung to the Lord and His word, Psalm 23.

My income decreased, but I knew the Lord would make a way. I knew that He didn't want me in a dangerous, toxic lifestyle.

So okay, now you know how everything started. What I thought would probably take only six months, lasted much longer. I drew my strength from God. It was like pulling out my fingernails, but it didn't kill me, and I'm sure it made my faith stronger. Malach 2:16.

The Restraining Order Appearance

September 5, 2010

T he day came when I had to face him about the restraining order.

I walked into the courthouse. They directed me to a door to my right. Opening the door was a large room with people sitting in chairs, with an aisle going down the middle. I showed the clerk my paperwork, and he directed me to sit in the section to the right.

I knew no one. As I waited, I observed the people in the room. No one in my section spoke to anyone across the aisle. I finally surmised the plaintiffs on one side, the respondent on the other.

As I sat there, my soon-to-be ex entered the room. He had shaved his head and was wearing a large cross necklace. His appearance scared me more than usual. I only guessed it was to intimidate me.

His lawyer approached me and said he wanted to speak to me. I replied, "I have nothing to say to you," which in turn my side of the aisle started to clap and roar in affirmation for my actions, as if to say, *Stick to your guns, girl.*

There was a table at the front of the room with a judge. It was very quick since so many were waiting to be heard. After brief questioning, they extended my restraining order and recommended we get a quick divorce and go our separate ways.

Again, I left the courthouse completely, mentally and emotionally exhausted, but thanking the Lord for taking care of me and keeping me safe, praying continuously this would be over soon.

Still, the day was not over. I had to find a lawyer, and I had to be quick.

The Lawyer

I had looked through the yellow pages for a lawyer. I had no idea how to pick one. I saw free consultation on one ad. Decision made.

That didn't work out so well. He told me that I would lose everything. He spoke to me as if I were a criminal and offered me no hope. After the consultation was over, I told him that I would get back to him, being pretty sure I would never step into that office again.

When I got into my car, I burst into tears, not knowing what to do next, but still full of hope remembering Isaiah 54:17: "No weapon formed against me can prosper."

After a few days had passed, I received a bill in the mail for nine hundred from that lawyer. When I called him, he explained that we had spoken longer than thirty minutes. That was not in the yellow pages ad. We discussed it, and he dropped all fees. Praise the Lord.

I decided a female lawyer might be a better choice. In the yellow pages, there were two to choose from. When I called the first one, the line was busy, so I called the second one. I made an appointment, answered some questions, and we planned to set a court date. She did tell me that the state I lived in usually rules unreconcilable differences, and everything is split fifty-fifty.

Before I tell you the rest of my story, I will tell you it took what seemed to me a very slow and agonizing process. The judicial system is oh-so-busy, and there was a lot of warnings, also a lot of praying.

Many times when I thought it was finished, my attorney would assure me it wasn't. It, for the most part, took thirteen months because my husband fought it every step of the way. He was determined to destroy me, but God had a better plan for me.

My First Court Appearance

August 31, 2010

I remember that morning I woke with dread. The thought of being in the same room with him again was gut wrenching.

As I waited at the courthouse for my lawyer to arrive, I prayed harder than I ever had before. I told God that my hope was in him only. It was just God and me.

When my lawyer arrived, she briefed me on what was to be expected, listing the possibilities of having to sell the house—which meant my dogs and I would have a slim chance of finding a place to live—possibly spousal support, losing 50 percent of my 401(k), and any other assets the court deemed valuable.

I remember as if it were yesterday what I said, "No, God is with me, and he will take care of me." Of course, she looked at me with those eyes as if to say, "You poor delusional thing." Believing it would not turn out any differently than other divorce cases she has represented. It was the law after all.

As I entered the courtroom, I could feel the intense spirit of hatred for me. He had hired the most outrageous lawyer determined to bury me alive.

My husband petitioned for the SUV, he did not want the Camaro. His attorney argued that he had a hard time getting in and out of the car. Then his attorney stated it had mechanical problems. My attorney argued that the SUV was bought for transportation for the dogs, which it was. The SUV was awarded to me and the temporary residency of our house.

He also petitioned for $700 monthly for spousal support, which I could have never afforded. He was awarded $378. The only reason he got spousal support was that my income was higher than his disability payments.

My lawyer said we did well and left it at that.

After court, I returned home again completely exhausted not feeling the victory. I feared somehow he would take revenge, but the Lord kept me safe.

Throughout the whole ordeal, I clung to Romans 8:28: "All things work together for good to those who love the Lord." He was all I had, and that was more than enough. No one could help me like he could. I had no friends or family nearby, but I was not alone; the Lord was my refuge, my rock.

September 1. I sent in my spousal support payment through the state, agonizing as I wrote the check, but God was in control, and I surrendered to that.

September 18. I drove to his lawyer's office where the SUV was parked, went in, and exchanged keys of vehicles. I was so relieved that part was over. Now if I had taken a dog to the vet, I had transportation. Amen.

October 4. Another petition came from the court. My ex wanted to pick up his personal belongings. I packed up all of his clothes and other personal items and put them on my front porch. A friend of his came to pick them up since the restraining order was still active.

January. As time went on, I had much contact with my lawyer. I had gathered all my information about our debt, house appraisal, cars, credit cards, my 401(k), and other assets. The list went on. What we were worth and what we owed, which was more. Then back to court again.

My attorney advised me that she and his attorney set up a mediation. That didn't happen. My ex was convinced he had me at his mercy. God promises to protect the lowly, and no one was more lowly than me.

This time, the court was a little different. My ex took the stand. He was still fighting to get the SUV and to increase the spousal support.

My attorney questioned him about the SUV, stating that it was bought for the transportation of the dogs.

"What did he expect me to do about them?" she asked.

He replied, "You can kill them for all I care!"

I gasp out loud in shock. He was the one who had adopted all of the dogs. I held back the tears, not even imagining he would say something like that.

By now my attorney was astonished. This doesn't happen this way in the court system. I retained the SUV, and the spousal support stayed the same. He was ordered to pay half of the credit card debt but got half of my 401(k). His attorney was rather shocked.

February. In February, we had to file a contempt of court because he had not paid his share of the debt. He also had not told his lawyer that he had received half of my 401(k). Since he owed his lawyer money, the Christ attorney was rather shocked.

It was ordered he had to appear before a providing judge of the family law department and then show to the court any reason why he should not be punished for failure and refuse to comply with the orders made by the court. I did not have to attend.

Time passed, and again we were back in court. My attorney warned me, prior to entering the courtroom, that we didn't have a chance. The presiding judge was known to showing no mercy to women and never judged in their favor. I told her, "No, I believe in my God, and he will take care of me." I meant that with all my heart and still do to this day.

As we entered the courtroom and sat down, the judge was giving his decision to the woman in front of me. I don't remember exactly what it was, but she was crying uncontrollably. She had lost. Fear tried to attack me, but I stood firm.

Just then a court clerk went up to the judge's bench, announcing the judge was overbooked, and we were reassigned to another judge—miracle.

We went across the hall to another courtroom. Both of our lawyers and we stood before the new judge.

If I've learned one thing, it is to never interrupt a judge when he is speaking. My ex obviously never learned that. He interrupted the judge. The judge slammed the gravel down, leaned into his face, and told him he would be held in contempt if he spoke one more word.

That day, my spousal support, which was to last five years, was reduced to $300 a month. I was to live in the house for now, and I got permanent ownership of the SUV.

God is so good. Fear not.

"Be strong and courageous. Do not be afraid or terrified because of them for the Lord your God goes with you, he will never leave you or forsake you" (Deuteronomy 31:6).

As time went on, I had to produce tax forms and pay stubs. During that time, his lawyer produced a list of furnishing that his client wanted from our home. It was five pages long, detailing every room of the house. At that point, I didn't care. Those things were of no value to me. They were a reminder of my past, and I was so ready to move on.

In April, his lawyer filed a motion for reconsideration. So the judge ruled to put a lien on the house. After ten years, if one or the other hadn't died, or I hadn't refinanced the house, I am to pay him $46,500. His lawyer also asked for a 4–5% inflation factor included, which the judge denied.

As the summer approached, I received more and more letters from my attorney.

The opposing attorney, to no avail, tried to get us to agree to change the ruling of the court. This curtailed forgiveness of credit card debt and extending spousal support, which was totally ludicrous.

He also wanted to schedule pick up for house items. I didn't agree to the request unless he paid his share of the credit card debt. Of course, he filed a contempt of court against me, and that meant returning to court once again.

He still said he hadn't received the money from 401(k) to pay the credit card debt, but little did he know that I had followed up with my 401(k) company and was able to get a copy of what they call a QDRP. He had already been paid by then.

He told no one of the 401(k), not even his lawyer, whom he owed money to.

The judge did not hold me in contempt but explained he would pay his share of the debt, and I would schedule a time for him to pick up the household items.

Also, I was awarded a quitclaim deed to the house, which meant I could change the title to the house in my name, which I did.

*****

Time doesn't stop, neither does the mental anguish. I never imagined this would drag on what seemed like an eternity. The Lord and I had spent much time together. I prayed for it to be over, always asking why is this dragging on? I cried a million tears, but I trusted him and knew he must have a plan.

September 23, 2010. It was the day of finalizing the divorce. I have heard that before, so I didn't have my hopes up.

That morning as I got ready, I prayed and prayed, begging God to let me know *why* I was being tortured like this.

I was kneeling in the middle of my living room floor and he told me!

We entered the courtroom, and proceedings began. The judge, out loud, reviewed all the rulings like we had done many times before. I was awarded the house, all debts were divided evenly, spousal support of $300 monthly was continued for five years from the date of filing, and the SUV was mine.

When the judge had finished, he asked if all parties agreed to the divorce. The other lawyer announced that my ex-to-be wanted to reconcile. This came as no surprise to me since his plan of destroying me had failed. I refused, and the divorce was finalized.

My ex left the courtroom, and his lawyer came over and asked if he could talk to me. My attorney said it was okay. He preceded to tell me his client still owed him money as if he expected me to pay the balance. I told him that was not my concern.

As my lawyer left the courtroom, we entered an empty elevator. Now it was time to give her a message from God, what he had told me.

I said her name. "You know I'm not a nutcase or anything, but I have to tell you something that God wants you to know He is trying to get your attention."

She replied "*I know.*"

About the Author

AJ was brought up with a religious background, only knowing God as someone to pray to when in trouble or asking for forgiveness. Therefore, her life was full of bad decisions, not even knowing that they were until it was too late. Later in life, she was introduced to the true God, Jesus Christ, and the Holy Spirit. It was a process of learning what her life was really meant to be about, how the Lord had always been there and always loved her, and that he wanted only the best for her.

CPSIA information can be obtained
at www.ICGtesting.com
Printed in the USA
BVHW040036110522
636524BV00052B/1155

9 781098 090883